Poems

by Gerald

Gerald Hatley

ISBN 978-1-0980-8712-8 (paperback)
ISBN 978-1-0980-8713-5 (digital)

Christian Faith Publishing, Inc.
832 Park Avenue
Meadville, PA 16335
www.christianfaithpublishing.com

Printed in the United States of America

Contents

The Shoot-out

Out here in Sooner land, and the Lone Star State
Where western men are as tough, as the Lord would make
There occurs each year, a war of raw will
That to this day still provides, an emotional thrill
When the Sooners and Longhorns, all gather around
To meet each other, at the State fairgrounds
Understand it is not a time, for meekly souls
To venture out, for pregame strolls
For flying through the air, you see
Is more than just the air you breathe
Sticks and stones, bricks, and bats
Cowboy boots, and Stetson hats
The battle begins, on downtown streets
And wages all night, until the dawn breaks
When the weary warriors, both orange and red
Wishing they had gone to bed
Hasten to their final goal
Their meeting place, called the Cotton Bowl
As the final hour, of this clash draws near
From the screaming crowd, you just might hear
Both Longhorn and Sooner yells
Hook 'em horns and go to hell
And even if you do not happen to be
For either of the teams, you are about to see
Your emotions will fill, with excitement and delight
The moment that ball, is kicked into flight
And after it is all over, said, and done
The best team has, usually won!

Gerald Hatley
October 8, 1975

My Place Called Home

There was this place, that I called home
So many years ago, I left to roam
Leaving lifelong friends, far behind
Looking for something, I needed to find
My how the years, passed so fast
As my travels took me, East to West
New friends I met, along the way
Many I still have, to this very day
Life was good, and I lived it fast
But then one day, as youth had passed
And my journey at last, almost at the end
Fondest memories, of where it all began
Consumed the thoughts, within my soul
As I come to realize, I am growing old
No longer young, enough to roam
I longed for the place, that I called home
Finally realizing, what I had left to find
Were all of the things, I had left behind

Gerald Hatley
March 2015

School on the Hill

There was this school, on the top of a hill
Where many of us went, and we love it still
We strolled those halls, with so many dear friends
Thinking those days, would never end
Then came the night we walked across the floor
With tassels and gowns, and out the gym door
A passage in our lives, had just come to an end
One we could never, relive again
Many lifelong friends, went separate ways
Not looking back, to the good old days
How distant to many, they must now seem
Almost as if, they were just a mere dream
Would we appreciate more if it were God's will
That we could relive, those days on the hill
But we know full well, that it cannot be

We can only look back, in our minds and see
How absolutely wonderful and blessed we feel
To have had our days, at the school on the hill

Gerald Hatley
April 2015

Home Guntersville

Nestled in the Alabama's rolling hills
Lies a small town, named Guntersville
Almost an island, with water everywhere
A place of beauty, beyond compare
Visited by de Soto, many years ago
When only trees, and weeds did grow
In the late 1700s, John Gunter became
The person for which, the town was named
His grandson Will Rogers, was famous we know
For history and legend, confirm it to be so
As years went by, with the passage of time
The dam was completed, in the year of '39
Giving birth to the lake, that we still use today
A place for those, who want to visit and play
The lake brought me, a great many smiles
As I fished the shoreline, running over eight hundred miles
The Gold Cup races, with loud engine sound
Brought almost a hundred thousand visitors, to our small town
Lee Taylor and his boat, *Hustler*, once came to our lake
The world water speed record, he wanted to take
In '67 Lee drove *Hustler*, to accomplish his goal
At 285.22 mph, the world record he did now hold
So Guntersville proudly entered the record book
See for yourself, go and take a look
Our history is rich, and memories abound
Of this wonderful place, that is our hometown
Just like the water, that under the bridge does flow
So do the years, with their many memories go
May the youth of Guntersville, live to hold true
The joy and memories, of the town we all knew

Gerald Hatley

Memories

A great gift from God, and so many we find
Is that of the memory, we hold in our minds
For when precious moments, have fled away
Never to be relived again, on some other day
Just as a computer, brings back to its screen
Our mind recalls memories, of long-past dreams
What would life be, if we could not recall
Moments from the past, so dear to us all
While it is very true, we can't live in the past
But is it so bad, to want memories to last?
As time passes by, for me it sure seems
Those memories from the past, are like sweet dreams
Bringing back the joy, I felt so long ago
When I lived them for real, and now I know
They will always be there, when I want to replay
My memories from the past, that I still cherish today

Gerald Hatley
May 5, 2015

Maui, Hawaii

As I stand upon the ocean's floor
Watching the waves crashing on the shore
My hair blowing in the offshore breeze
Palm leaves crackling high in the trees
Native Mynah birds making strange sounds
As they search for food around the grounds
The sweet smell of plumeria fills the air
Their trees full of blooms seen everywhere
The sun paints a brilliant aura in the sky
As it sets in the horizon and darkness is nigh
Conch shells proclaim the end of day
As daylight fades so slowly away
Another day soon comes to an end
But soon the cycle will begin again
When golden rays beam from the sun
Sending the darkness again on the run

May 17, 2015

The Seasons of Life

Isn't it strange as we grow old, to look back at life and see?
Memories that before were not understood, but now seem clear as can be
Seasons we have taken for granted, now take on a brand-new theme
Reminding us of our life, in ways we have never before seen
Birth is like the springtime, when everything is so new
Trees bringing forth new leaves, and flowers blooming too
Even the birds are building nests, preparing for the day
When new-laid eggs ultimately hatch, as new life finds its way
But spring is a tender time, as new life must for now depend
On those who brought us into this world, until our summer days begin
Oh, and all those summer days, how wonderful were they?
We learned to walk, run, and play, and did so almost every day
We met so many new friends, our days were so full of good fun
How we wished the nights would end, and the next day had begun
But soon it was off to school, the learning days were here
We had to spend our days in class, with teachers in our ear
For many long years the summer season, seemed without an end
But soon this season goes its own way, and a new one does begin
The fall of our life, with school all gone, we now are fully grown
Having to work and support ourselves, for we are now on our own
Those comfort days with Mom and Dad, have long since passed away
Most of our time we spend at work, with so little time to play
We seldom reflect on tomorrow, and what the next day will bring
We live each day of our lives as if it were an endless string
Then suddenly we realize that fall has reached its end
September has gone, days are growing cold, as winter does begin
We look into the mirror, and much to our surprise
The person looking back at us, we do not recognize
The winter of life has finally arrived, and so many things now seem
To change with each day that passes, and we are never quite the same
Muscles grow weak, vision is dim, the skin has many wrinkles

Leaves fall from trees, birds fly away, eyes have lost their twinkle
But as the season is closing in, on what will be our last
We give thanks to God above, for our life and all of its past
But are there things we would change, that happened along the way
Or say to someone, if only they could be with us here today
My final prayer is my heart will open, and my feelings will find their way
Into the hearts and minds of those, I wish I could talk to today

Gerald Hatley
August 6, 2015

Ray LeCroy

The year was around 1949, and I was just a young lad
The scout hut was new, the playground was open, and kids were
    extremely glad
For it was the place where friends could meet, to play and have some
    fun
I would go there almost every day, to swing, to climb, and to run
My friend Sammy and I would meet, along with many good friends
We played each day and had so much fun, until the day had to end
Two softball teams would be chosen, that daily a game would play
Mrs. Wood appointed a captain for each team, their names I recall
    today
Guy Whitaker and Ray LeCroy, were picked to lead the scene
They would choose from the other kids, to fill out both the teams
Captains chose their players; we were lined up by the scout hut wall
With each selection chances grew slim, that I would play at all
Only a few younger kids not chosen, remained against the wall
Knowing the chances were very thin, that we would receive a call
My face told a story as tears began to swell; I knew it was just not to
    be
Then Captain Ray LeCroy looked my way, and said, "Kid, you can
    play for me"
My heart beat fast, a smile came upon my face, the tears all went
    away
Ray LeCroy became my hero, and he still is to this very day
Ray did not know the joy he brought to me, for at least some fifty
    years
At the Chorba and Lee recognition day, with many gathered near
I told the story to Ray, which he heard for the very first time

Tears of joy came down his face, and words he sought to find
But the face and not the words, tell the feelings from the heart
The same way my face told it, that most beautiful day at the park

Thank you, Ray, I shall never forget

Your friend,
Gerald Hatley
August 16, 2015

My Favorite Season

The trees tell me, it is that time of the year
That I love so much, and hold so dear
The time for school, to start again
And students to be, with all of their friends
The hint of fall weather, fills the air
Leaves are turning colors, everywhere
Fireplace smoke, curls from chimneys above
The aroma of burning wood, suggests warmth and love
The hills are ablaze, flaming colors in full view
The lake reflecting images, of the colored hills too
The lights at the stadium, are in full glow
It is Friday night; the team is ready to go
Of all God's seasons, given us to behold
To me, fall is the most wonderful of all

Gerald Hatley
September 5, 2015

Goodbye to Sue

Where are the words, that we want to say?
To portray our dear friend, we celebrate today
Where are the words, that are so difficult to find?
To create a clear image, of her in our minds
The image of happiness, and that beaming face
That genuine smile, of friendship and grace
How does one make, the brush strokes disclose?
The portrait of this person, we want to expose
The words a masterpiece, would truly display
The image of one dear to us, God has called away
Perfect words are, sometimes challenging to find
To reveal the real story, that one leaves behind
The more beautiful the person, like this one we knew
Makes finding the words, even more difficult to do
For I can never recall, a time nor a place
When there was not that smile, upon her face
Joy and happiness, those who knew her know
Always accompanied her, wherever she would go
But there comes a time, when we all must say
Goodbye to someone special, we met along life's way
For chapters in our lives, surely come to an end
Sometimes we wish, they were only about to begin
But we can find comfort, heaven is a more joyful place
Having this beautiful new angel, and her beaming face

Gerald Hatley
September 12, 2015

Holiday Wish to a Friend

I truly do love, this time of the year
As the holidays to me, are so very dear
My sorrow and troubles, drift far away
As happiness and cheer, do fill my days
The world just seems, like a better place
Friendly smiles seen, on many a face
Decorations and colored lights, in plentiful display
Proclaiming the seasons, are on their way
A time to give thanks, and wish abundant cheer
To those we have chanced upon, over many a year
For it is all too often, we neglect to convey
Those things in our heart, that we mean to say
May peace and joy, abundantly make their way
Into your life, for the remainder of your days
And though our lives, may have been estranged
My memories and friendship, have never changed
May your holiday season, be full of happiness and cheer
May health and good fortune, follow you throughout the year
May the memories and our friendship, forever be true
Hope you think of me with fondness, just as I think of you

Gerald Hatley
October 22, 2015

Looking Back

As I stand upon, the hands of time
Looking back over, this life of mine
Scenes appear, from years long past
Happy am I, that they still last
Some not thought of, for a long time
But aged and priceless, just like fine wine
Removal of the cork, and they are released
To recreate the scenes, that have been unleashed
My soul fills, with both happiness and joy
As I recall scenes, from when I was but a boy
So many faces, in the mural appear
Some still with us, many no longer here
But I cannot look away, from the mural I see
For faces looking back, were all friends to me
They helped make my life, what it is today
God blessed me, when they all came my way
My prayer for you, is that you too may recall
A mural of life, projected in your mind's wall
And I hope and pray, that facing you
Is my face smiling, as a friend to you

Gerald Hatley
November 16, 2015

Christmas Memories

So many memories, so very dear
So much happens, this time of year
Waiting for Santa, with toys and sleigh
Trying to sleep, while he made his way
Jumping out of bed, at dawn's first light
To find the presents, he left last night
It was so pure, and innocent back then
Never to be the same, later on again
The Christmas parade, on downtown streets
Waving to good friends, we love to greet
Christmas carols and ads, on the movie screen
Gave a personal touch, to our local scene
Lights and decorations, were seen everywhere
Smoke from chimneys, curling through the air
Everyone seemed happy, a smile on every face
Many good friends, seen all over the place
A Merry Christmas greeting, and a hug or two
Brought smiles of cheer, and warmed hearts too
Yes, those were the memories, may they not fade away
May our hearts and minds, relive those days
May you find happiness and faith, in so many ways
May you still get excited, as Christmas draws near
And may you live Christmas, each day of the year

Gerald Hatley

To Our Friend, Tom

We first met Tom, not very long ago
Our friendship it seemed, was destined to grow
We did so many things, and had many great times
But something was missing, that Tom wanted to find
Someone to love, and to hold as his wife
Was that something that Tom, was missing in his life
We had known Miss Donna, for quite some time
And invited her and Tom, to our home to dine
We brought them together, in hopes they would find
Something that would bind them, together for all time
Thinking back at that night, and the days that came to be
Their love grew strong, and most everyone could see
But all was not roses, there were obstacles to overcome
And together they overcame them, one by one
We witnessed their wedding, at a beautiful holy place
Happiness and joy, visible all over their face
A human metamorphosis, occurred that beautiful day
As Tom and Donna, had finally found their way
Out of suppressed darkness, that kept true happiness concealed
The love felt for each other, a new life was revealed
Light from the Heavenly Father, could be seen in their face
As we left the wedding ceremony, at that holy place
The love between them, was so evident and so pure
There was never a doubt, that it would always endure
It was only two short years, they would ultimately share
But the quality of those years, was beyond compare

It is hard to accept, but we must try every day
To cope with life, when one so loved is taken away
We must trust in God, and let him take our hand
Knowing full well, he will lead us to our Promised Land

Gerald Hatley
January 25, 2016

Happiness Lost

As the days draw near, for life's final years
So many memories come to mind, so truly clear
Way back to my childhood, when I was just a lad
I can remember the friends and fun, that I had
Life was so simple, when compared to today
We had no cell phones or computers, to substitute for play
Few had money, or material things to share
But friendship and joy, seemed almost everywhere
Red Rover come over, and kick the can
Were games we played, till darkness and Mom called us in
Friendships were formed, from daily contacts we shared
Not from internet strangers, that pretended they cared
Trust and freedom were very real, love and happiness ruled
Political correctness was something, yet to be schooled
The internet did not exist; social media was unknown
My how things have changed, now we have grown
So many things very prevalent, to every one of us today
Could be so life enhancing, if used in a positive way
Think of what an educational tool, the internet could become
If children could roam free, without all of the scum
Privacy and solitude were possible, in that day
No cell phone calls, and the ringing sounds they play
As great as some inventions, may seem to be
Some cause problems, for you and for me
Yet the younger generation, takes it all in stride
Life must have been boring, back then they chide

But we know the happiness, our generation was dealt
And watched as like snow, on the mountain did melt
Perhaps never by anyone, to be enjoyed again
As we did long ago, when we played kick the can

Gerald Hatley
March 2016

Clear Your Heart

Be careful as you, walk life's path
To live each day, as if it's the last
When it comes, it will be too late
To express regrets, you wanted to relate
Words you should have said, long ago
Words you wanted, someone to know
Held very deep, within your heart
That misplaced ego, would not let you start
To discuss differences, from the past
That should be forgotten, too trivial to last
Pebbles that became boulders, what a shame
To turn a good life, into a foolish game
And now the game, can never end
That will let a new life, begin again
So do not let pebbles, get out of hand
Check that ego, as soon as you can
Communicate feelings, if differences exist
Work them all out, never let them persist
Life's path is too short, do not take the chance
Eliminate the pain, and enjoy the dance
For the joy of life, can never be denied
If you have someone you love, still by your side

Gerald Hatley

Remember When

It was long ago, but can you remember when
We said the pledge, before class could begin
Merry Christmas was expected, way back then
Replacing Christ with X, was considered a sin
Happy holidays was something, we did not know
But then, my dear friends, it was a long time ago
So many changes, from years gone past
Things we took for granted, would always last
And here we are wondering, how could this occur
So many things changed, from the way they were
Who gave the orders, for this evolution to begin?
How long will it continue; will it ever end?
If we remain complacent, letting others impose
Their desires over ours, as we act with repose
Where will we be, in a few short years
Our children living, in our most dreaded fears
Those who would change us, we must defeat
Political correctness, must die at their feet
All lives matter, both white and black
We must all unite, and take our country back
Support of our military, and law officers too
Must be something, that we agree to do
Anarchy and crime, cannot be allowed to exist
United we can stand, and together we can resist
We must understand, there are serious trends
If not confronted, our America will surely end
Behind the scenes plans, are being carved in stone
Based on us not united, but standing alone
If you love America, and want to return
To that better place, for which we yearn
Then study the candidates, and what they say

They will accomplish, as president of the USA
Choose wisely for we, must elect the one in the race
Who truly loves America, and will lead us to that place.

Gerald Hatley
2018

A Political Point of View

Is it just me, or has my mind gone astray?
That I cannot fathom, the way things are today
It seems an attitude, of give it to me free
Pervades the thinking, of so many that we see
Certainly the disabled, should be cared for every day
Misfortune not invited, happened to come their way
Lack of work for many, and no place for them to turn
They deserve to be cared for, until once again they can earn
But I believe our Christian teachings, and trying to relieve the hurt
Are being used against us, by those who just do not want to work
Foreigners cross our borders, illegally day and night
Looking for jobs and handouts, or to join the terrorist fight
Does our government not care; all those funds they spend
Comes from citizen taxpayers, to help our country mend
Our country was not intended, to be ruled by executive decree
We have a House and Senate, to look out for you and me
It seems they too have chosen, to look away or turn a deaf ear
Rather than to support the wishes, of those who voted them here
I think I speak for many, who believe we have had our fill
Our country cannot sustain, much more that causes all this ill
For it is in God we trust, and the country that we once knew
When people worked together, and so did our government too
America is more important, than all of our selfish plans
Our Christian way of life must once again, be the rule throughout
    our land
And those who cannot accept, our American way and God's plan
We wish you well and say goodbye, as you leave in search of another
    land

Gerald Hatley
May 4, 2016

A Wish Fulfilled

The Tiki Warrior completed, his daily evening run
Children following at his heels, having so much fun
One by one each lamp he lit, much to the children's delight
The fire from each of the tikis, turned darkness into light
Now the many flames flicker, so gently in the breeze
Birds seeking a place to roost, high among the trees
Daylight begins to fade, as the sun is setting low
Another day is coming to end, as darkness continues to grow
Peggy and I sit in the garden, so she can have a smoke
We watch the many geckos, and listen to them croak
We see an endless stream of vehicles, slowly make their way
People arriving at our hotel, just starting their holiday
While others depart in sorrow, their holiday now at end
Having to return home wishing, it was only about to begin
Their holiday in paradise, has for now come to an end
Another may be in their plans, in the future I suppose
For Peggy and I, the sorrow runs deep, although our hearts will yearn
The illness in her body, will no longer allow her to return
Back to this tropical paradise, where we spent many wonderful days
Enjoying the tropical breezes, good food, and her golden rays
Returning here one last time, was a desire she dreamed to fulfill
I did have doubts about her physical strength, but none about her will
She was so strong and determined, I knew she would make it through
With total support from Heather and Gerald Jr., her final wish came true
I will for the rest of my days thank God, for this blessing that he gave
Granting Peggy peace and happiness, for at least a few more days

Gerald Hatley
July 2017

Speak Your Heart

Why don't we tell someone so dear, our thoughts they surely should know?
Why do we suppress them deep in our minds, and never let them go?
So often our hearts and minds, will not allow our words to ever reveal
The body closes up shop, and the mouth cannot express how we feel
Thoughts we hide deep in our minds, where they do not belong
Perhaps the fear of appearing weak, in a world expecting us to be strong
Maybe it is just too much pressure, for some to risk all the pain
Do we not see the healing they might be, or the joy to be gained?
Instead we muddle along each day, the benefits dying in our minds
They get buried so deep in the archives, that soon we can no longer find
Then one day the unexpected takes place, and we have to face the cost
The words and feelings went unsaid, and the potential happiness is lost
So now those words will never become, happiness to someone's ears
Now all that is left is our empty heart, and a face with many tears
A lesson to be learned for some, if the words should ring true
And this one thought if you will allow, I want to leave with you
Be kind and thoughtful to all you know, and in everything you do
So tears you shed are tears of joy, that come from happiness in you
Shed not the tears of sorrow, that portray the color of blue
For those tears are tears of sadness, that came from inside you

Gerald Hatley

The Pendulum of Life

How I long for the days, when happiness did abound
But now it seems they are gone, and nowhere to be found
The pendulum of life swings to and fro, and we never know
What lies in the direction, the next swing will surely go
So many routines we live each day, without a second thought
Taking for granted all the importance, and happiness they brought
But when they are no longer, to fulfill our lives each day
Their absence leaves us empty, and darkness finds its way
Into our daily being, and the many things we like to do
Which seem now somewhat, hopeless and even irrelevant too
And yet we know life goes on, and we prepare the best we can
Yet wishing there was a way, to relive some past days again
We wonder if we did our best, could we have done a lot more
To engender a life of happy feelings, contentment and full of joy
There is no reverse in the pendulum of life, time keeps moving ahead
Time to thank the Lord above, for all the things we have had
The pendulum swings to winter, and our days are growing short
Now is the time to engage life fully, no time to think, *Abort*
The past is gone and the books are closed; nothing more we can do
But some of life still lies ahead, that we must grasp and hold on to
Following the swing in winter, we do not know what our life may bring
But always know when winter is gone, the pendulum swings to spring

Gerald Hatley
November 2017

Time Seems to Fly

The calendar indicates, the holidays are drawing near
How can that be, didn't we just celebrate a new year
When we were young children, I seem to recall
Those days we wished for, seemed always to crawl
Slower than Christmas, were the words most often used
To describe our disgust, for the time that was abused
For the days seemed to pass slowly, would they ever arrive
If they did not come soon, how could we even survive
But as the years have passed, and we have grown old
The speed of light, seems now to have taken control
Everything around us, seem to be caught in the race
Except for our bodies, which now can't keep pace
Once we laughed at old folks, who moved so slow
Now we hear the laughter, wherever we now go
I just cannot believe, time has passed so very fast
Why couldn't it have gone slow, as in youth's past
It is too late now, there is nothing that can be done
Just get a stiff upper lip, and try to have some fun

Gerald Hatley
November 2017

A Christmas Wish

May you be happy this time of the year.
May your lives be filled with joy and cheer.
I pray you have all that you need to survive.
May your hearts be pure and your spirit alive.
May you be kind to others lending a helping hand.
That helps them feel good whenever you can.
May you try for the rest of your natural days.
To make every day Christmas, giving God all your praise.

Merry Christmas
Gerald Hatley

To Kelly

I can't believe, how the years have passed
But so many memories, will always last
How you would cry, when I had to leave
Your day care sitter, was not nice I believe
It hurt me so, that I asked to take control
And watch you each day, as our lives unfold
Gymnastics and kindergarten, together we went
So much time together, we happily spent
There was a time, though you never knew
My main reason for living, centered around you
Now that high school graduation, is almost here
It is off to Alabama, for your freshman year
And though I will miss you, more than you know
It is vital to your development, that you go
The next few years, will be the happiest you may live
But you need to remember, that you too must give
Care and kindness, to those you will get to know
So the bond of friendship, will continue to grow
Be an example to others, serve Christ every day
So you won't have to worry, as you travel life's way
I am here for you, for as long as I may live
But you must be strong, to handle what life may give
Thanks for the memories, I cherish them with pride
Good luck at Alabama, and a big Roll Tide

I love you so very much, Poppy
May 6, 2018

Thoughts of Remorse

Sometimes a light turns on, within our heads
That brings to bare some of the things, we once did
Things at the time, that seemed okay to do
But looking back now, seem disruptive and unkind too
Were we just too young, to fully comprehend
Or too shallow minded and selfish, to care how it would end
I think of the time, and opportunity we did waste
That could have been spent, putting smiles on a face
As we now grow old, and look back over the years
Some of our past memories, can bring back tears
Many are gone, whose pardon we would bid
So we ask the Lord to forgive us, for what we did
And wonder why we never were able, to see the light
And find answers to questions, in the "Book of Life"
What a treasure chest available, to embrace our minds
If only we had taken the opportunity, to seek and find
And now that our final season, is assuredly close at hand
We should grasp at truth, in every way we can
Remembering that Jesus, died on the cross
To forgive our sins, so our souls would not be lost

Gerald Hatley (MCHS Class of '56)
July 16, 2018

My Eightieth Birthday

I can still recall, when I was a young boy
My entire hometown, was my own personal toy
I could fish, I could run, I could climb the tallest trees
Always on the go, and very happy to be
Playing games with friends, at the local park
Seldom getting home, much before it was dark
Back then I would jump out of bed; I couldn't wait
To get out of the house, and head for the lake
My best friend Sam and I, a vow did make
To always be friends, and to stay in shape
The friendship vow, was easy to hang onto
But staying in shape, was just too hard to do
So as you can now see, standing before you
A vow was lost, and staying in shape was too
Today as I awake, from an unrestful sleep
I ease out of bed, and cautiously to my feet
For if I hurry, and try to proceed too fast
I usually fall on the floor, and bust my ass
Sleeping through the night, is a wishful dream
My bladder wants up, several times so it seems
As soon as I stand up, gravity starts to check-in
As feet and legs, start to swell once again
The titanium hip, in my right side says "stop"
As I try to bend over, to put on my socks
I can still lace my shoes, if all goes as I intend
If not, my stomach, seems to shut off my wind
Removal of cataracts, played a major share
In elimination of all that haze and fog, in the air
A new world has surprisingly, opened all around
With all the new sounds, my hearing aids have found
The snap, crackle, and pop, we use to greet

Came from the cereal, we were about to eat
Those sounds are now, from cartilage and bone
Letting us know, they want to be left alone
Sometimes entering a room, I have to stop and stare
And ask myself, "Why the hell did I come in there"
The grey matter frequently, now takes a break
And leaves me clueless, for goodness' sake
I sometimes bump into a friend, at the grocery store
Whose name I can't find, in my memory anymore
If I go out to repair something, in the lawn
I take a cane, and my cell phone along
For if I should slip, or have to get down on the ground
I can't get back up, and if there is no one around
I can scare off any critter, with the cane in my grip
Until I can use the cell phone, to call for help
I am so happy to see all of you, and oh by the way
Can someone please tell me, why you all came today

Gerald Hatley, 2018

Trends of Caution

There are so many trends, that continue to come down
As the earth we call home, continues to spin around
Trends that first move slowly, compared to a glacier's crawl
That gently covers the area, like a shadow on the wall
When large enough to catch the eye, the reaction is total surprise
How could this possibly have occurred, right before our eyes
Culture change is not well received, if it is pushed too fast
Those desiring changes know, evolution will work the best
Subtle changes barely noticeable, are often put into play
That pave the road for others, planned to come our way
Eliminating the pledge of allegiance, and saying prayers in school
Removing God from money, are nothing more than tools
To slowly change the way we feel, and prepare us once again
For even more severe changes, that propagates the plan
Removing the Ten Commandments, from the courthouse hall
Denying Christmas manger scenes, in the public malls
Part of calculated plans, the politically correct to please
A truly significant effort, of bringing America to its knees
America alone stands in the way, of the "one world order" ruse
Christianity must be weakened, in order for them not to lose
Weaker military and gun control, are already part of the plan
To reduce the ability of America, to help defend our land
Conspiracy theory some will say, but winds of evolution blow today
And the glacier's snaillike move, will surely continue to creep
Until America's freedom, no longer will we be able to keep
Unless we fully trust in God, and his help continue to seek
We could fall like the Romans; complacent, immoral, and weak

Gerald Hatley, 2016

Together

No need to complain
About anything today
We will take whatever
May come our way
For at the close
Whatever may be
I will be with you
And you will be with me

Gerald Hatley
June 8, 2019

Expression of Feelings

Rarely is it difficult, for me to find
Words that create, some kind of rhyme
But now I am somewhat, at wit's end
To think of the words, that I want to begin
That tell the feelings, deep within my heart
I search for them, and where I should start?
The story I want to relate, should reveal
The deep feelings, my soul does conceal
Feelings of love and respect, so very sincere
Directed at someone to me, so uniquely dear
Why do I hesitate to express, how I truly feel?
The feelings are sincere, and very real!
Do I feel they would be rejected, or misunderstood?
How does one relate honesty, and truth if one could?
Into words that are kind, heartfelt, and true
That create happiness and warm feelings, in you
I can only hope that my message, is crystal clear
And lets you know I hold you, so very dear
May the words bring warmth, happiness, and cheers
To someone I want to be close to, for the coming years

Gerald Hatley
Jan. 3, 2019

Valentine Day Wish

If the good Lord left it, up to me
And I could choose, the one to be
My valentine, for all time to come
It would be so easy, to choose the one
That would fill me up, so full of pride
And others with envy, they cannot hide
For they know full well, it is so very true
Just like me, they too would choose you

Gerald Hatley
February 2019

Truth in the Mirror

I can only speak for myself, and not about you
But my guess is that you, feel the same way too
When I open my eyes, to the morning light
And arise from my bed, with great delight
Knowing another day, has made its start
I am thankful to God, that I too will be a part
Of this miracle of miracles, that is called life
Propelled by past memories, both fond and of strife
I eagerly prepare, for the events of this day
Happy to take on whatever, may come my way
My mind projects youth, infallible without end
Capable of performing, just as it has always been
Walking to the closet, to pick out some clothes
I feel the numbness, in my feet and toes
A little reminder, some changes are real
And old father time, is still trying to steal
My eternal youth, that my mind surely knows
Will always be there, the years will forever expose
Tomorrow comes to some, but certainly not to me
I will always be young, and eternally age-free
Continuing to get dressed, to face another race
I stop at the mirror, to ensure all is in place
Suddenly stunned, at the image that I see
Who is this person, looking back at me?
The face is aged, the back is hunched
His midsection reflects, way too much lunch
My mind explores its database, a match to reveal
To identify if this mirror image, is truly for real

I am filled with reality, as the identity is now clear
That my own self has changed, by many a year
Realizing the fact, that youth is no more
I prepare for whatever is left, that life has in store

Gerald Hatley
February 3, 2019

Expression of Love

I pray I can express, the words that convey
The feelings of my heart, for someone today
Perhaps they will be mistaken, or misunderstood
Creating rejection and distrust, not acceptance and good
I believe that special feelings, of love can persist
Not driven by desire and passion, that may exist
An honest feeling of love, so real and sincere
Felt within your heart, for someone very dear
You want to do for them, rather than them do for you
Patience and understanding, in you must be true
For deep warm feelings, so often take time
Imbedded deep within our minds, that firewall filters must unbind
It is tragic and sad, but so often turns out true
Feelings of love with good intentions, never pass through
Doubt and mistrust, encountered in the past
Seem so hard-bitten, that they tend to last
Causing doors to hearts, not to open too wide
That allow feelings very real, to come in and reside
Opportunity for a relationship, built on a true love
So perfect it could have been, ordained from above
Floats silently away, as if caught in the wind
Maybe never to return, our way ever again

Gerald Hatley
February 7, 2019

My Brother Sam

I had this friend named Sammy; we were so very close
We were more like brothers, or so it seemed to most
In summer when school was out, we would always be together
Riding our bikes all over town, regardless of the weather
We hiked the hills, and explored a few caves
Looking for Indian relics, from long-ago days
We would arise early in brutal cold, it would still be in the night
Into the woods we would go, hunters awaiting daylight
You could hear the squirrels, moving carefully in the trees
As Sam and I got ready, a trigger we would gently squeeze
Thanksgiving Day in 1954, before the Albertville game
Sam and I went hunting, our nerves in an effort to tame
When we were very young, our first basketball game we played
After the game I ask Sam, how many points he had made
"Six points," he replied, "four for us and two for the other team"
Arising early on Monday morning, to Val Monte we would go
Lots of golf balls in the shallow water, for us to find you know
When we first arrived, the water would be very clear
We could see the balls on the bottom, that
we gathered up with cheers
Soon the water would become muddy, and we no longer could see
What lay there on the bottom, so we felt around with our feet
We stopped harvesting golf balls, from Val Monte at the lake
The day I almost stepped on, a large water moccasin snake
Once the high school paper, in the Chatter column did state
That Sam and I were going steady, what laughter that did make
Our friendship lasted throughout the
years, until we both were grown
Then Sam's heart gave out, and one day suddenly he was gone
I do wish Sam could be here today, the stories he could unwind

But we must be content to remember him,
in our heart and in our mind

Gerald Hatley
May Sam, Myrtle and Bud,
my second family, rest in peace

The Book of Life

The book of our life, is the manifestation of God's creative power
The pages are memories, describing how
we lived the life he endowered
We all have memories, we would like to erase
We all have memories, we love to embrace
But all of God's works, were done with intent
Not by chance, but they all were meant
To provide us with knowledge, of the tribulations we will face
As we proceed through this life, preparing for a heavenly place
The road will be narrow, and only a few will find the gate
While the road to destruction, is wide and straight
Be steadfast and focused, on the task at hand
Life is not a video, and cannot be replayed again
We have this one life chance, to prove we are worth
The price paid by Jesus, while he was on this earth
Spend the rest of your life, with one thing in mind
Seeking the narrow road, with the gate hard to find

Gerald Hatley
November 29, 2018

The Houseboat

Every September, for thirty years or more
Several couples would travel, to the lake's shore
Early years to Trinity, and later Shasta Lake
We packed for the party, a full week it would take
Two houseboats we rented, with five couples each
Left the marina, in search of a suitable beach
Securing the boats, with long stakes in ground
We then searched, for firewood scattered around
The nights were cold, and the fire blazed when poked
We sat drinking wine, and telling lots of good jokes
Mornings started with coffee, and a tropical fizz
Followed by a breakfast, best described as gee-whiz
Cleanup then followed, a long time it would take
Then pull up the stakes, and head out on the lake
Ladies went on top deck, claiming to get some sun
Actually seeking relief, from all the drinking they had done
Very slowly we cruised, as fishing lines were out
Bait running very deep, where the big boys hung about
Fishing pole tips watched, with a passionate wish
Hoping for an eruption, when bait was grabbed by a fish
Smallmouth bass, and lots of lake trout
Were the most common fish, that we pulled out
By early evening, a new spot we had to locate
To secure the boat, and swim in the lake
Then break out the booze, let the party begin
Knowing that tomorrow, we would do it all again
We had Sea-Doos and ski boats, as a change of pace
And we used them to fly around, all over the place
Sunday mornings were special, there was football to play
Most guys went to the marina, to spend the day
The girls were left alone, for which they were glad

Without us about, was the most fun they had
A big screen TV, beer and Bloody Marys too
We arrived about ten, and got picked up around two
Lots of male bonding, at the bar did transpire
And by the end of the day, we could not be any higher
So many stories, I would like to relate
Of the many events, that took place on the lake
By far the most wonderful memories, I will ever recall
Are the times we spent together, great friends all

Gerald Hatley
February 8, 2019

To Carol (a.k.a. Debbie)

We were college sweethearts, some fifty-seven years ago
Our lives went different directions, and
without any contact to know
Where the other lived; married, single, or even if alive,
No contact occurred with one another,
but our memories did survive
One evening as I sat alone, this beautiful person came to mind
Was she still alive, was she happy, how on earth could her, I find?
And would her mind still hold fond memories,
of our college campus days
Would she even talk to me, and forgive my foolish ways?
Then one magical evening, her voice was on the phone
I knew from the moment I heard it, my lonely days were gone
Just when you think life, has all but paced itself out
And you reconcile yourself, with lots of inner doubt
Someone comes along, creating an enormous explosion
Giving life a new meaning, stirring up all your emotions
You feel like youth has returned, with the
excitement you once knew
You cannot wait to get up each day, this life to start anew
To think that at my age, this metamorphosis could even take place
Makes me want to sing God's praises, and thank him for his grace
Now here we are together, as if never having been apart
Older and hopefully wiser, we have more than created a spark
A raging fire of emotion, now lives within our hearts
That exhilarating feeling, that long ago I knew
Is in my heart yet again, to help me make it through
What will be the closing chapters, of my life on earth

I can now look back with heartfelt thanks, for all that it was worth
So many beautiful memories, forever depicted in my mind's wall
But none with greater prominence, than
the night of the "Carol call"

Gerald Hatley
May 2019

Thanks to Charlie

As we grow old, it sure seems to me
We appreciate things more, that used to be
A message I received, from a longtime friend
Got me to thinking back, all over again
Our past holds memories, of times we had
That now when remembered, we may feel sad
Sad they are only memories, there in the past
How great it would be, if they could forever last
Classmates that we, may never again see
Football games where, we celebrated victory
Friends so scattered, all over this land
And we haven't a clue, how to reach them again
How fortunate for some, who still recall the past
These moments of pleasure, don't ever pass
They remain in our hearts, and in our minds
Of the beautiful life, that time left behind
Personally I am filled, with thoughts from long ago
Of events and friends, that I will never let go
So, Charlie, I thank you, for the message you sent
Recalling a wonderful time, that we spent
With coaches Chorba and Lee down on that field
Where many memories were born, may we always feel
We're major contributors, for who we are today

For those were truly happy days, and I can honestly say
My life was so enriched, by those who passed my way
May God bless every one of them, each and every day

Gerald Hatley
July 26, 2019

Special thanks to Charles Wallace for his thoughts and especially his friendship.

A Tragic Loss of Life

My granddaughter told me a story, while at lunch one day
A tragic story that somehow, had made it her way
A sheriff department's employee, had been fatally shot
While providing security, at a campus parking lot
Like many people who hear bad news, we too felt very sad
After thinking for a moment, I spoke to her and said,
"We cannot know the sorrow and grief, or truly understand
The feelings many people felt, who really knew this man
We hear of these events that happen, often very far away
For a brief moment we feel sad, but then go about our day
But what about the mother, who lost a child she once had
Or children who learn about, the loss of their mom or dad
The hurt and pain that is so intense, we simply do not feel
But sadly, all that grief and pain, for many are very real
Perhaps God intended us to be touched, in a shallow way
For what would life be, to feel that much pain every single day"
Not a day goes by on this earth, that someone's life is not gone
Someone who was loved by many, who are now left alone
Maybe a sense of sorrow, is all we're expected to feel
For one we never met or knew, is all our emotions can reveal
But we should remember, there are those that in that life did dwell
That now are going through agony and grief, their life now in hell
I propose in future days, a prayer we always remember to make

That ask for forgiveness and salvation, for those that evil takes
And grant peace and understanding, to all those left behind
With what now is only memories, of a loved one in their minds

Gerald Hatley
September 24, 2019

This is dedicated to Mr. Dornell Cousette who lost his life defending
the University of Alabama while on duty. He served our country in
both the military and in police work. May God take him into heaven
and grant him peace and rest. We all should thank him for his ser-
vice to our country and our community. Rest in peace, Dornell, and
thank you for all you did.

Christmas Is Past

Christmas has yet again drifted, into that space we call past
And for many of us the drift, was simply too fast
Gone now are the decorations, and the Christmas trees
Not as many smiles, on the many faces we see
It is now back to the grind, of everyday living
Thoughts now evaporated, with the joy of giving
Why is this so, we should ask ourselves
Is Christmas only about, reindeer, sleigh, and elves
Should we not look deeper, for the true meaning of the day
The existing celebration is certainly, not the way
That was intended, I believe, on that cold Bethlehem morn
When in a manger, inside a stable, a child was born
The birth went unnoticed, with exception of a few
Some shepherds tending flock, and some wise men too
Yet here we are today, over two thousand years have passed
And the story of Jesus, in our hearts, sure seems to last
While the story of Christmas, was given birth that same night
The true meaning of the day, has also drifted out of sight
But we can take refuge, without any doubt in our mind
That Christmas came about, to save all of mankind
Still with us today, and will be so until the end of days
When all evil will be subdued, and good rewarded for its ways
Yes, Christmas should be celebrated, each day or the year
And we should give thanks, for the one we hold so dear

Gerald Hatley
January 10, 2020

In Honor of Two Great Men

My life, like so many others, took shape and mold
Due significantly to two men, who in my heart I hold
So fondly with gratitude, for the influences they implanted
Into my heart and soul, so I took not for granted
The sweat and blood, their actions brought out
Left us tired and exhausted, but there never was doubt
That we were being prepared, for things yet to come
Things that would live past, the time when we were young
The transition between youth, and fully grown adults
Was bridged by these two, with outstanding results
They never gave up on us, as we were tempted to do
But always stood strong, so as to see us through
Yes, thanks to Coaches Chorba and Lee
Over twelve years they set a record, for all to see
A hundred wins, twenty-three losses, and six ties, history does show
But those of us who played for them, truly know
If both were still alive today, they would surely proclaim
Their greatest success, is how their boys played the game
The stadium in Guntersville, that bears their names
Reminds us how they prepared us, for all of life's games
The saying, "When the great scorer comes to mark against your name
It won't be if you won or lost, but how you played the game"
They taught us to play the game, as it was meant to be
May we, if we live, make them proud, for all to see

Thank you, Coach Chorba and Coach Lee I hope you know what
you mean to me.

Gerald Hatley

A Different Easter

The sun will rise, and the day will begin
Just as it has, since way back when
It is Easter Sunday, but unlike those you know
No sunrise services, for Christian folks to go
No children dressed up, in their Sunday best
Will be hunting for eggs, in their usual quest
Church will be empty; no one's there to hear
About Jesus arising, leaving the tomb bare
Like the Passover, in Bible days of old
With lamb's blood, over the door we are told
God's people had, to remain at the home inside
While death roamed through, the world outside
Now we too are confined, and shelter in place
As the coronavirus spreads, all over our space
Causing sickness worldwide, and much death too
Could it be an indication, being sent to me and you?
That there is an unrest, in our heaven above
Regarding our actions, on this earth that we love
We believe this crisis will end, to the relief of us all
But if change doesn't happen, will the next shoe fall
And would it be more severe, than what is here now
What can we do, to prevent another and how?
That I cannot answer, but each one of us should
Ask ourselves questions, being honest if we could
Am I living my life, in a Christian way?
Do I try to do something good, for others every day?
Do I truly believe there is a heaven above?
Do I feel God's Holy Spirit, and his undying love?

If the answers we give, are honest with some disbelief
A search of the scriptures, may provide some relief
Yes, Easter this year, may be altered and strange
But the message of the cross, will never be changed

Gerald Hatley
April 11, 2020

My Life Cycle

As I sit in my home, and wonder where
All the years went, that are so very dear
Childhood years, so vivid to me still
Thinking of them now, provides a thrill
A love never ending, of those precious years
So much happiness, and so few tears
Many reasons required, that I moved away
From my own hometown, and go my way
For time goes on, and life brings about change
I adapt to the new, but it still feels strange
Fear and uncertainty, often took control
Until I adjusted, as my new life unfolds
Then one day, my comfort zone reappears
And I muse to think, of those needless fears
Those previous changes, unleashed for a while
That are behind me now, and again I smile
Then events take place, and once more I move on
To an unknown place, that I must soon call home
Those same fears and uncertainty, now back in mind
But not with the same intensity, as in previous time
For I have grown, and know I can endure
I have become self-sufficient, and know for sure
The challenge I can handle, and loneliness cure
But how many times, will this cycle repeat?
How many adaptations, will I be required to meet?
Where will I call home, there have been many to date
Friends left behind, as I move from state to state
My childhood home, where sweet memories abound
Could I live there again, in that wonderful town
Or has it changed so, from the place I used to know
That my memories and reality, would conflict so

I could not find peace, and contentment there again
And my loving memories of there, would come to an end
Life brings a mixture, of happiness and pain
And decisions must be made, that help us retain
Our most cherished memories, that forever be clear
To help provide us comfort and joy, in our final years

Gerald Hatley
May 19, 2020

A Fall Obsession

A sense of excitement, is swelling in the air
You can feel it growing, almost everywhere
Camps and campuses are, opening their gates
Getting ready to receive, today's football greats
The aroma of pigskin and analgesic, permeates around
The sweet smell, of fresh cut grass now abounds
Soon stadium lights, will illuminate fields with stripes
And the sounds of cheers, will be loud in the night
As hometown warriors, like gladiators of yore
Move the ball down the field, in their attempt to score
For those who have played, this remarkable game
The excitement and joy, each year are the same
We wait for several months, for fall to arrive
Eager to watch, how this year's team will survive
Then as quick as a flash, the season has passed
We hope and pray, that it will not be our last

Gerald Hatley
June 19, 2020

An Opinion

I guess it is safe to say, and certainly I
    hope it imparts that way
That none are offended by the words, this
    little prose attempts to portray
And whether or not you believe, in what
    the Bible content does express
I hope you will read this not as fact, but
    simply as one person's best guess
My affirmation to you is that I do believe,
    and I do so entirely by conviction
I have no knowledge or visions to share,
    that are undeniable connections
History has recorded many illustrations, of
    eroding moral values and beliefs
Ending predictably, in so many instances,
    to downfall, conquest, and grief
History does seem to repeat itself, now
    the cycle swings in our direction
Will we recognize this slow evolution,
    and seek to stop its progression?
Words from the late President JFK, have
    never been more relevant
"Ask not what your country can do for you,
    but what you can do for your country"
It seems that many today, have forgotten
    the president's request
They appear to be going about, doing
    what for themselves is the best
We see it on the streets, and on the TV every day
Buildings being burned; looting and
    violence now seem to be the way

They want to take our guns; we are told
    they just are not safe to own
But if they get away with that, how
    can we defend our homes?
Do not mistake what is going on, that
    it is only due to chance
This effort is highly organized, and appears
    now to have reached advanced
Remember not long ago, when Merry
    Christmas was not to be portrayed
The manger scene and the Ten Commandments,
    were not to be displayed
Now we see police attacked, and told
    to stay out of the way
Their budgets slashed, manpower
    cut, much to our dismay
Demands for the National Anthem to be
    replaced, where does it all end
It will not stop or slow down until we
    rise up, and finally take a stand
Our country that most of us love, where
    freedom and justice really live
May be on the brink of destruction, unless
    we confront the immoral will
And if we fail to meet this need, and turn
    the socialist progression away
Our way of life may be lost, and not
    see light from another day

Gerald Hatley
July 2020

The Changing World

I sit looking out my home office window, at the landscape view
Thinking about days gone by, and the wonderful times I knew
Thoughts center on my hometown, my life's start had just begun
Just a young kid I was back then, too naive to know anything but fun
What a wonderful time to launch a life, and in a country strong and free
Life was simple way back then, or at least so it seemed to me
But there are many, if you ask today, who would surely have another view
Two different worlds existed then; one black, and the white one I knew
I do not think as youths we knew, and certainly did not understand
Why segregation was the rule, practiced throughout our southern land
It was a way of life, we had been taught from the day we were born
Acceptance was the only stance, it was perceived to be the norm
Now as I look out my window, with eyes that are growing old
I now make my own decisions, and ignore many things I am told
I no longer see people being forced, to the back of the bus
I no longer see people being branded, as something less than us
We have finally come to accept, though it did take too long
That previous way of life we lived was, in the eyes of God, wrong
But now these old eyes do perceive, a malicious attempt and goal
Premeditated on fundamentally replacing, this republic that we hold
As the greatest form of government, and country ever known
With an oppressive collectivism, that free people could never condone
The wedge being driven today, between those who are black and white
Is nothing more than a deception, for the left to replace the right
And if you think your individual rights, regardless of the color of
   your skin
Are of any concern to those supporting this change, you better think
   again
We must accept that time has come for all, both black and white
As God's children, put our past aside, and unify in this crucial fight

About the Author

Born in Guntersville, Alabama, Gerald spent his childhood and early school days there. He subsequently graduated from the University of Houston with a degree in optometry. Never establishing a practice in optometry, he joined IBM and spent his entire working career in information technology. His career took him from the east to the West Coast with stops in Texas. He loves sports, especially football, and enjoys fishing. He was married to his late wife for fifty years prior to her death in 2017. He has one son, Gerald Jr., and a daughter, Heather. He has five grandchildren.

CPSIA information can be obtained
at www.ICGtesting.com
Printed in the USA
BVHW081203290321
603635BV00003B/251